Vocabulary Villa
Become a Grammar Guru

Rachna Chhabria

Published by
Renu Kaul Verma
Vitasta Publishing Pvt Ltd
4348/4C, Ansari Road, Daryaganj
New Delhi - 110 002
info@vitastapublishing.com

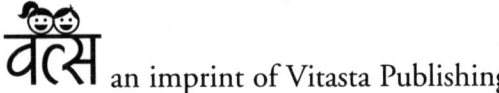 an imprint of Vitasta Publishing

ISBN 978-81-19670-59-8
© Rachna Chhabria
Illustrations © Vitasta Publishing
First Edition 2024
MRP ₹299

All Rights Reserved.
No part of this publication may be reproduced, stored in a retrieval system, or transmitted in any form, or by any means—electronic, mechanical, photocopying, recording or otherwise—without the prior permission of the publisher.

Cover Design by Somesh Kumar Mishra
Illustrations by Val
Layout by Rohit Gautam and Saumya Chaudhary
Edited by Kangam King
Printed at Chaman Enterprises, New Delhi

FOR ANIL NICHANI

Jiju, your silent support means a lot

CONTENTS

Introduction	vii
Meeting the Magical Letters of the English Alphabet	1
When Mr Slang Came Visiting	10
Tree of Knowledge and Fruit of Wisdom	17
The Dwarves of Punctuation	25
A Trip to the Zoo	34
Learning to be Chefs	42
Homing in on Homophones	50
Howzat Homonyms	56
It's Raining Metaphors	62
You Said It	67
Amazing Alliterations	72
Personifications are Fun	80
Writing Prompts	90
Acknowledgements	93

INTRODUCTION

When Geeta Menon, the Editor of *Children's World Magazine* (a Children's Book Trust publication), reached out to me in 2019 to do a column for the magazine, she had just one criterion, whichever topic/theme I chose, had to have continuity, as it would be spanning over ten months.

I decided to write ten stories, creating a set of characters who would take children through the different aspects of grammar and language in a fun and easy manner. The result was the column called Grammar Guru and the three characters – Aman, Rakhee and Roshni. Grammar Guru tackled one aspect of the English Language in each issue. The goal was to help readers discover the Grammar Guru in them. As children, most of us find grammar and essays a daunting subject. I chose this theme to help children navigate the world of grammar so that they don't fear it anymore.

Though I am no expert, I have ensured to the best of my abilities that everything I have written is accurate. The stories have been whetted by several experts – an English teacher as well as a few writers.

The first few stories may seem too simple for older readers, but after that, the stories switch tracks and both younger and older readers can enjoy them. Actually, anyone young at heart can enjoy them.

My column Grammar Guru was published in *Children's World Magazine* from January 2020 to December 2020, barring April and November. It was published in Volume LII, Nos 1,2,3,5,6,7,8,9,10 and 12.

The previously published stories have been rewritten for the purpose of this book.

The last two stories have been written solely for this book. I have also incorporated a few word games at the end of each chapter. The thirty writing prompts at the end of the book will enable readers to explore their writing skills.

1
Meeting the Magical Letters of the English Alphabet

'MAMA, TELL US a story,' the nine-year-old triplets Aman, Rakhee and Roshni said. Mama was sitting on the sofa in the airy living room, reading a book. Reading was Mama's passion, and she had a vast collection of books.

The children stared at the cover of their mother's book. It was the latest bestseller. They also loved reading, a habit they had inherited from their mom.

Roshni had long black hair and a round face with wide-spaced brown eyes. She was older than her siblings by a few minutes. Aman was the middle child. Thin and short, with eyes that seemed a little large for his small square face, he had wavy black hair which he combed several times a day. Though Rakhee was the youngest, she was also the tallest. Her oval face always had a cheerful look and her large brown eyes sparkled like gems. Her short hair, with a tendency to curl at the edges, was tied in a high ponytail.

Mrs Priya Menon, the triplets' mother, taught English Language in their school, but for the senior grades. Tall and thin, their mother took care of her fitness, eating healthy food and exercising daily. It was no wonder then, that her skin always glowed and her eyes sparkled. Mama's hair was long and thick. Her favourite scrunchie held it together in a ponytail. It also matched her pink and blue kaftan.

The children were always hungry for stories and Mama never lost an opportunity to teach her children the different aspects of the English Language through stories. Their father Mr Sunil Menon was in the Navy. He was away for long stretches of time. When he returned, he too regaled his children with wonderful stories full of his travel adventures.

'Once upon a time, there were twenty-six magical elves. They were the letters of the English Alphabet. Their names were A, B, C, D, E, F, G, H, I, J, K, L, M, N, O, P, Q, R, S, T, U, V, W, X, Y and Z. They lived in a big house called Alphabet House. As there was no one to look after them or teach them anything, the elves constantly fought with each other, arguing, creating trouble and throwing tantrums. One day, Lady Language, a gentle and kind-hearted soul, walked past their house. She took an instant liking to the house and the elves,' Mama said.

Reclining comfortably on the smaller sofas, the children listened keenly. They had closed their colouring books and placed their crayons over them. Hearing the words magic and elves, their eyes sparkled and their bodies trembled with excitement.

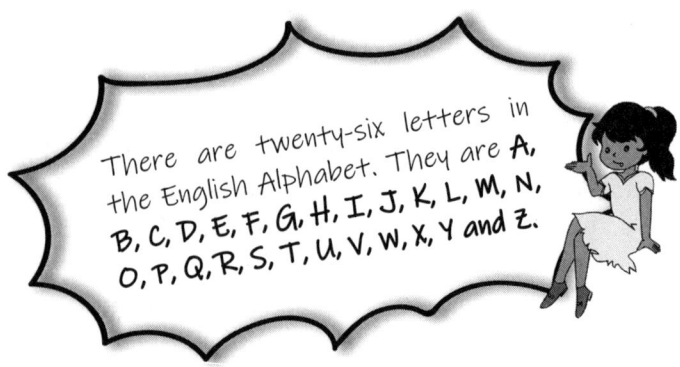

There are twenty-six letters in the English Alphabet. They are A, B, C, D, E, F, G, H, I, J, K, L, M, N, O, P, Q, R, S, T, U, V, W, X, Y and Z.

The only sound in the room was made by the grandfather clock. Tick tock. Tick tock.

A couple of sparrows had alighted on the guava tree in the garden, announcing their presence with chirps.

'Then what happened?' Rakhee asked. Fond of the colour yellow, she was dressed in a tee shirt and shorts of that hue.

'The friendly lady looked at the shabby house with its rundown garden, windows covered with grime, and the equally dirty elves. The elves looked skinny. They had long and bony faces, smudged with dirt and unkempt hair. They wore unwashed and crinkled clothes and scuffed shoes. Lady Language was neatly dressed in a light purple gown, with not a strand of hair out of place.'

The children stared at their mother and listened silently. Even the birds had stopped chirping.

'Lady Language felt sad and decided to help the elves. She arrived at Alphabet House every morning. She cleaned it, removed the weeds from the garden and watered the plants. She urged the elves to have a bath and cooked delicious food like noodles, vegetable cutlets, grilled sandwiches and pasta for them. Lady Language was friendly and kind. All the elves loved her,' Mama said. 'She gifted them sweaters with their names on them. The elves always wore her handmade cardigans.'

'Lady Language sounds like a sweet person,' Rakhee smiled.

'She was,' Mama replied.

'What happened after that?' Aman asked. His blue tee shirt and shorts had small red stains. At breakfast, he had dropped tomato ketchup on his clothes.

'To make Lady Language happy, the elves started having a bath every day. They also helped her clean the house,' Mama said as she inserted a bookmark inside the book she was reading. 'They asked her to live with them and she agreed. Slowly they started mimicking Lady Language's behaviour. And before they realised it, they had stopped fighting and arguing.'

'Like us?' Roshni asked. She wore her favourite black and white striped dress. Her freshly washed hair was open.

'You all fight sometimes,' Mama rolled her eyes.

'I fight only when these two gang up against me,' Aman gestured towards his sisters.

'We fight only when Aman gets annoying,' his sisters replied.

Mama shook her head. She hoped the children wouldn't start arguing.

A crow cawed from the branch of the mango tree. A couple of dogs barked in the street.

'One day, it rained heavily, and the entire garden was flooded with water. The elves watched the rain from their rooms. When it stopped raining, birds, butterflies and squirrels appeared in the garden. The dark clouds disappeared. Drops of water clung to the long grass, birds twittered and the squirrels chattered.'

'It must have been a wonderful sight,' Rakhee sighed. She loved squirrels and butterflies and wanted to keep them as pets.

'It was,' Mama said. 'A few letters,[1] U, N and S, came out of the house to play. At first, they played separately,

---

[1] Henceforth, the elves will be just called 'letters' to give the story a better flow

splashing through the puddles and chasing butterflies around the garden. Lady Language, sitting on the porch, watched them. She was knitting new sweaters for them. Soon they started playing together. Holding each other's hands, they ran around the bushes and jumped over the puddles. As the game progressed, they rearranged themselves and formed the word SUN. Instantly, a merry sun emerged from behind the clouds.'

'Wow,' the children said excitedly. They exchanged delighted looks. This story was becoming more and more interesting.

'Their carefree laughter and noisy games attracted the other letters. They too joined them in the garden. Everyone wanted to play the word game. As the letters W, I, N and D played together, it became windy. The leaves rustled and the tall grass swayed in the breeze. When the letters C, L, O, U, D and S chased each other, small clouds filled the sky,' Mama continued. 'Lady Language was delighted as the letters were creating magic with their games. They were also having a lot of fun.'

'I would have loved to watch the letters play,' Aman laughed.

'The letters also realised something,' Mama said.

'Can any of you guess what it is?'

'That they didn't hate each other anymore,' Rakhee replied.

> **Vocabulary** means all the words in a language or all the words someone knows. When we say that someone has an amazing vocabulary, we actually mean that they know a lot of words.

'Yes, but they understood something else too,' Mama said.

'That they were magical?' Aman and Roshni said together.

'Yes,' she grinned. 'The letters realised that they were magical. That they had the power to multiply. Every time the letters nodded their heads, a few more letters jumped out of their body. When they shook their heads, the extra letters disappeared into their body.'

'Cool,' Rakhee said.

'I would love to have that kind of magic in my body,' Aman sighed.

'We can't tolerate more than one Aman,' Roshni shuddered.

'Just imagine how much three Amans would eat,' Rakhee laughed. 'We would always be starving then.'

Aman scowled at his sisters. He was a big foodie; his sisters always teased him about it.

'The letters now played new word games every day. One day they made a long word RAINBOW. A beautiful rainbow appeared in the sky.'

The children had a dreamy expression on their face. They had many things in common; besides stories, they loved rainbows and clouds.

Mama looked fondly at her children. 'The letters also realised that when they were alone, they were useless. But, if they played together, they could create magic. They had become so fond of each other that soon caring and sharing became a part of their nature.'

'Like us,' Aman put his arms around his sisters' shoulders.

Mama nodded.

'The letters played every day, forming big groups and small groups. Nodding and shaking their heads to make duplicates, they created many different words, which slowly started spreading through the world,' Mama went on.

'Didn't they get bored?' Rakhee asked.

'No,' Mama replied. 'They were forming new words every day. One day, Lady Language told them that now it was time to play a different game. Can you all tell me what the new game was?' she asked.

'The Game of Sentences,' the children screamed.

'My clever kids,' Mama smiled. 'O, U, L, V, E, I, O and Y played together and made the first sentence for Lady Language. Can you guess what it was?'

'I LOVE YOU,' Rakhee, Roshni and Aman said together.

'Yes,' Mama's eyes shone with excitement. 'Lady Language told them that five of them were special. Guess which five?'

'A, E, I, O and U,' the triplets answered.

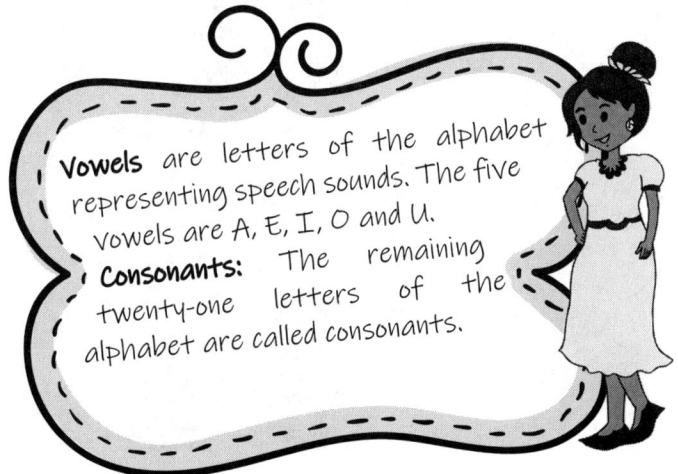

Vowels are letters of the alphabet representing speech sounds. The five vowels are A, E, I, O and U.

Consonants: The remaining twenty-one letters of the alphabet are called consonants.

VOCABULARY VILLA

'And why were they special?' she asked.

'No word or sentence game can be played without these five special letters. These special letters are called vowels,' they replied.

'As the letters made more and more words, Alphabet House came to be known as Vocabulary Villa. Its fame spread far and wide. People from all over the world heard about it,' Mama ended the story.

Roshni had a smile on her face, as though she was watching the letters play their games. Aman started sketching a small house, while Rakhee drew an elf. Mama returned to her reading.

Outside the window, a few sparrows started chirping.

Word Games

1. Make your own Vocabulary Villa. First, draw a large house. Keep a timer near you. In sixty seconds, write inside the house twenty words that share the first alphabet of your name. Alternatively, you can use the first alphabet of your surname. Now describe yourself using those words.
2. Take a big word; for example, periwinkle, consultation, conundrum, university, anthology, ubiquitous, or any other word. See how many smaller words you can make from the big word in two minutes.
3. Learn a new word every day and make a sentence using that word.
4. Word *Antakshari** is a fun game. The game starts with the first person saying a word. If the first person says the word 'goat', then the next person's word must start with the last alphabet of the first person's word. In this case, it will be T. So if the second person says 'truth', the third person must say a word starting with H. If they say 'Heaven', then the fourth person's word must start with N. The game continues like this and the person who is unable to say a word is out of the game.

---

* Antakshari is a popular Indian musical game that involves participants singing songs starting with the last letter or syllable of the previous participant's song.

2
When Mr Slang Came Visiting

AMAN, RAKHEE AND ROSHNI had completed their homework by Saturday morning. Their Mama was in her favourite place in the living room on the brown single-seater sofa, knitting a sweater for their Dad. Excited to know what happened next in Vocabulary Villa, they approached their mother.

'Mama, please continue the story,' Rakhee said.

'Okay,' Mama placed the knitting needles on the low centre table. 'Mr Slang, a homeless man, roamed the streets every day. He had long shaggy hair and an equally long beard. His clothes were torn. On his feet were shoes that had several holes. One day he came across Vocabulary Villa. He liked the house a lot, as it looked neat and inviting. The moment he tried to enter the house, Lady Language, the prim and proper governess of the letters, sent him packing. This angered old man Slang.'

'What did he do?' Roshni frowned. She couldn't imagine the kind and gentle Lady Language being hard on anybody.

'Although Mr Slang left the premises, he kept a constant watch over Vocabulary Villa. One day, Lady Language went to visit her relatives for a few weeks. Grabbing his chance,

Mr Slang landed up outside Vocabulary Villa and settled down in the garden.'

'Then what happened?' Aman asked. His main worry was that Mr Slang shouldn't steal something from Vocabulary Villa.

'Initially, the letters didn't bother about Mr Slang as they were busy amongst themselves,' Mama said. 'But at night, when it turned cold, they saw Mr Slang shivering in the garden in his tattered clothes. Taking pity on him, a few of them opened the door and asked Mr Slang to use Lady Language's bedroom until she returned.'

'Oh no,' Roshni said. 'Did Mr Slang look after the letters like Lady Language?'

'No, he didn't,' Mama replied. 'Within a few days, all of Lady Language's hard work, disciplining and nurturing was whitewashed under the influence of this evil wizard. He refused to have a bath or brush his teeth and never combed his hair. There were even cobwebs in his hair. As for his clothes, they stank.'

'I feel so bad for Lady Language,' Aman looked grim. He had taken an instant liking to this gentle lady who had adopted the letters and taught them so many nice things.

'Mr Slang was known for his mischief-making ways. He slowly turned the letters against each other. He told the vowels that they were special, that word and sentence games couldn't be played without them. He convinced them about the extra magic in their bodies and he also brainwashed them into not sharing a room with their siblings. He asked them to demand special rooms for themselves.'

'That was so mean of him,' Roshni said. She loved sharing her room with Rakhee. Tucking her hand into her sister's arm, she leaned her head on her sibling's shoulder.

'Within three days of Mr Slang's entry into Vocabulary Villa, the letters started fighting. They were back to their old behaviour. The vowels now considered themselves superior to the other letters and refused to participate in word and sentence games. They constantly hung around Mr Slang.'

'That must have been disastrous?' Rakhee looked tearful. She was feeling sad for Lady Language and also for the letters.

'It was,' Mama said. 'When the letters played the word games without the vowels, the words lost their meaning. The earlier GOOD MORNING became GD MNNG. CLOUDS became CLDS. The word games were no more fun. Instead, they had become boring. No one understood the new word games anymore. As for the Game of Sentences, it was completely forgotten.'

'Lady Language must have been furious when she returned,' Roshni said. She had opened a packet of chocolate biscuits and shared it with her siblings.

'She was,' Mama nodded. 'Word travelled far and wide that Vocabulary Villa had once again fallen to ruins. Lady Language immediately rushed back. When she saw the state of the house and the fighting letters, she was disappointed. Mr Slang bossing around made her angry. But the strong lady made a plan to outsmart the old wizard.'

'What plan?' Aman asked. He was eyeing the packet of biscuits in his sister's hands. He had devoured his share and was hoping for more.

'Lady Language first filled the cellar with food, water, a mattress and blankets. Then she took the letters D and M into confidence, asking them if they would be a part of her plan by hiding themselves in the cellar at night. They instantly agreed and left a note for their siblings. The next morning, she announced to everyone that the letters D and M had run away, as they were tired of all the fights.'

'Super plan,' Roshni smiled, munching on her second biscuit.

'It was,' Mama said with a wink. 'Initially, the other

letters weren't concerned about their absent siblings. But, by afternoon, they started missing them. Joining forces, they searched the house, the garden and even the entire lane for their siblings.'

'The letters must have regretted their fight?' Rakhee said.

'They did,' Mama replied. 'They started blaming Mr Slang for it. They also felt bad that he wasn't helping them search for the letters D and M.'

'In the evening, it started to rain heavily; thunder and lightning struck the sky. The garden was flooded with water,' Mama continued. 'All the letters got together and taking torches and umbrellas went in search of their siblings.'

'Sweet of them,' Roshni smiled. She would have done the same if Aman and Rakhee were missing.

'The letters were getting worried as the minutes passed,' Mama said. 'They were also getting irritated with Mr Slang. He just wasn't bothered about the fact that his mischief had led to the disappearance of their siblings. When they approached him for help, he told them that D and M weren't important. This angered the others. Lady Language watched with a smile on her face as the letters chased Mr Slang out of Vocabulary Villa.'

'Old man Slang must have got a shock,' Aman grinned. Though he fought with his sisters, he also patched things up with them quickly.

'Yes, he never expected that the letters would drive him out,' Mama said. 'Somehow Lady Language pacified everyone. That night none of them slept due to anxiety and worry. The next morning, before they woke up, Lady Language got D and M out of the cellar. The other letters were overjoyed to see them. They ran into the garden immediately. When E, E, B, R, Z and E played together, a gentle BREEZE swept through the garden. When S, I, D, B and R held hands, different birds alighted on the branches, singing their sweet songs. Lady Language continued her knitting, assured that the letters had learnt their lesson and would never fight now.'

Roshni handed the leftover biscuits to Aman, who devoured them in seconds. A silence fell over the room as the children removed their clay set from a cupboard in the living room and started making small elves with the different coloured clay. Mama resumed her knitting.

Slang is a type of language that consists of words and phrases that are regarded as informal and are avoided in formal writing.

Word Games

1. Write a sentence using words that have just two vowels. It could be any two vowels. Choose the vowels beforehand. If I choose vowels A and E, then I have to make a sentence that has words with only these two vowels in it. The sentence has to be grammatically correct.

For Example:
Vowels chosen: **A** and **E**. Sentence: She was healthy, wealthy and clever.
Vowels chosen: **I** and **O**. Sentence: This silk skirt is torn.
Vowels chosen **I** and **U**. Sentence: I will visit his hut.

2. This next game can be played during birthday parties. A word is chosen. For example, Train. Children or the participants must say a word associated with the selected word. For train, it could be station, tracks, passenger, food, travel, engine, bogie, holiday, journey and so on. The person who comes up with the most unique associated word wins.

3
Tree of Knowledge and Fruit of Wisdom

IT WAS A Sunday afternoon. Aman, Rakhee and Roshni were in their parents' room, playing Chinese Checkers, a game gifted to them by their mother. Mama was sitting on a chair at her desk, her laptop opened, doing the accounts of the family-owned shop which sold all kinds of gift items. A manager handled the day-to-day affairs. Mama visited the shop every day after school and on Saturday mornings to check the items on display. She was constantly adding newer products, making the shop a much sought-after destination for all gift items. Her laptop screen was filled with numbers.

'Mama, we want to know what happened in Vocabulary Villa after the wizard Mr Slang was thrown out by the letters.' Aman asked. This story had become his favourite. He was constantly thinking of the letters. The triplets were sitting on the carpet playing their game.

Mama was pleased that her children had also started playing word games, just like the letters. She often heard them playing word Antakshari when she moved around the house completing her chores. She smiled whenever she saw them underlining a big word they read in the newspaper and searching for its meaning in the dictionary. They had also started borrowing books from the school library to read over the weekend.

Mama looked at them; they were growing up so fast. She was sure Rakhee had grown an inch taller in the last week. Roshni's dress looked small for her now. It barely touched her knees. Aman was the same. 'The letters had now realised that they could only play games if all of them played together. Their strength lay in unity. Alone, they were all incapable of creating anything new,' she said.

'That's so true,' Rakhee said. 'They had learnt a lesson they would never forget.'

'They did,' Mama agreed. 'As the letters continued to play together, creating new word games, a plant sprouted in the garden of Vocabulary Villa. Initially, it had just a few tiny leaves. One thing amazing about this plant was that it had different shaped leaves. Lady Language and the letters were enchanted with this unique plant. They would go near it every day to admire the leaves.'

'Under Lady Language's care, the plant started growing fast, spreading its thick branches in all directions. The different shaped leaves grew bigger. Soon it became a large tree with several branches sprouting all over. The letters would play around this tree daily. Lady Language sitting under its shade watched them with a satisfied smile on her face. They all felt a strange attraction to this tree,' Mama continued.

'What was the name of the tree?' Roshni asked. The guava tree in the garden was her favourite. It attracted a large number of birds and squirrels. She loved watching them.

'As no one had seen a tree like this before, they didn't know its name,' Mama replied. She was fond of gardening and had a green thumb. On weekends, she loved pottering

around her lawn, pruning the hedges and trimming the flowering plants. Their beautiful garden had won several prizes. 'People came from far and wide to admire this wonderful tree. Every morning, before the letters woke up, Lady Language would study the tree. She noticed that new branches and leaves were sprouting overnight. She realised that every time the letters played word games, more leaves appeared on the tree.'

'That's so cool,' Aman smiled. 'I wish the seeds you planted in our garden yesterday would become like this special tree.'

'For that, we have to play word games in the garden, just like the letters,' Roshni laughed.

'Lady Language named it the Tree of Knowledge,' Mama's eyes twinkled.

'I was going to call it the Dictionary,' Rakhee giggled, 'as the tree grew every time the letters made a new word.'

Wisdom means the ability to make good judgements based on what one has learned through experience. It also means the quality or state of being wise.

BECOME A GRAMMAR GURU

'Soon a profusion of fruit appeared on the Tree of Knowledge,' Mama said. 'And just like the leaves, fruit of different shapes appeared on its branches.'

'Wow,' Roshni exclaimed. 'Were they tasty?'

'They were delicious,' Mama replied. 'Lady Language named them the Fruit of Wisdom. As the fruit grew, both in size and number, Lady Language had no alternative but to distribute them among the people, as they were slowly filling up all the rooms in Vocabulary Villa.'

'That was generous of her,' Rakhee said.

'If you remember, I told you that Lady Language was a kind-hearted woman,' Mama smiled. 'Sharing and caring was her nature. Every morning she stood under the tree supervising the plucking of the fruit so that it didn't get damaged. She also made it mandatory that the first fruit of the day must be cut in Vocabulary Villa and eaten for breakfast.'

'Super,' Roshni's eyes sparkled. 'I'm sure eating the Fruit of Wisdom for breakfast made the letters wiser.'

'It did,' Mama said. 'Even when the letters jumbled themselves up, like B, K, O, O, without making a proper word, people realised that it was BOOK. Or when the letters, H, O, S, L, C and O played together, people knew that the word was SCHOOL.'

'Cool,' Rakhee's eyes shone with pleasure. 'I love this Jumble Game.'

'Here goes,' Mama said. 'B, L, E, C, S, A and O, R, S, O, U, H, M, S, M.'

It took the triplets just a few seconds to unjumble the letters. 'CABLES and MUSHROOMS,' they replied together.

'Let me continue the story,' Mama said. 'Soon smaller plants similar to the Tree of Knowledge sprouted all around Vocabulary Villa. Lady Language allowed the villagers to take these saplings home. Within a short span of time, every house in the village had a Tree of Knowledge in their garden. They in turn passed the new saplings to other villages.'

'That's such a wonderful thing,' Aman exclaimed. 'That way Lady Language ensured that both the Tree of Knowledge and the Fruit of Wisdom reached every corner of the world.'

'Yes,' Mama agreed. 'Knowledge cannot be kept under lock and key. It should always be shared. The more Lady Language spread the knowledge, the more it grew. The original tree had now stretched its branches all over the house.'

'Did any birds sit on this tree?' Roshni asked.

'Yes,' Mama answered. 'Small and colourful birds often perched on the branches of this special tree. These were the Birds of Imagination. Every time these birds came, Lady Language noticed that the letters played really creative games. The Birds of Imagination made their nests in the branches of the Tree of Knowledge. Lady Language knew that soon the letters would start playing the Game of Stories.'

Leaving Mama engrossed in her accounts, the children tiptoed out of the room, carrying their Chinese Checkers board with them. They planned to make peanut butter and jam sandwiches to surprise their mother. It was her favourite, and theirs too.

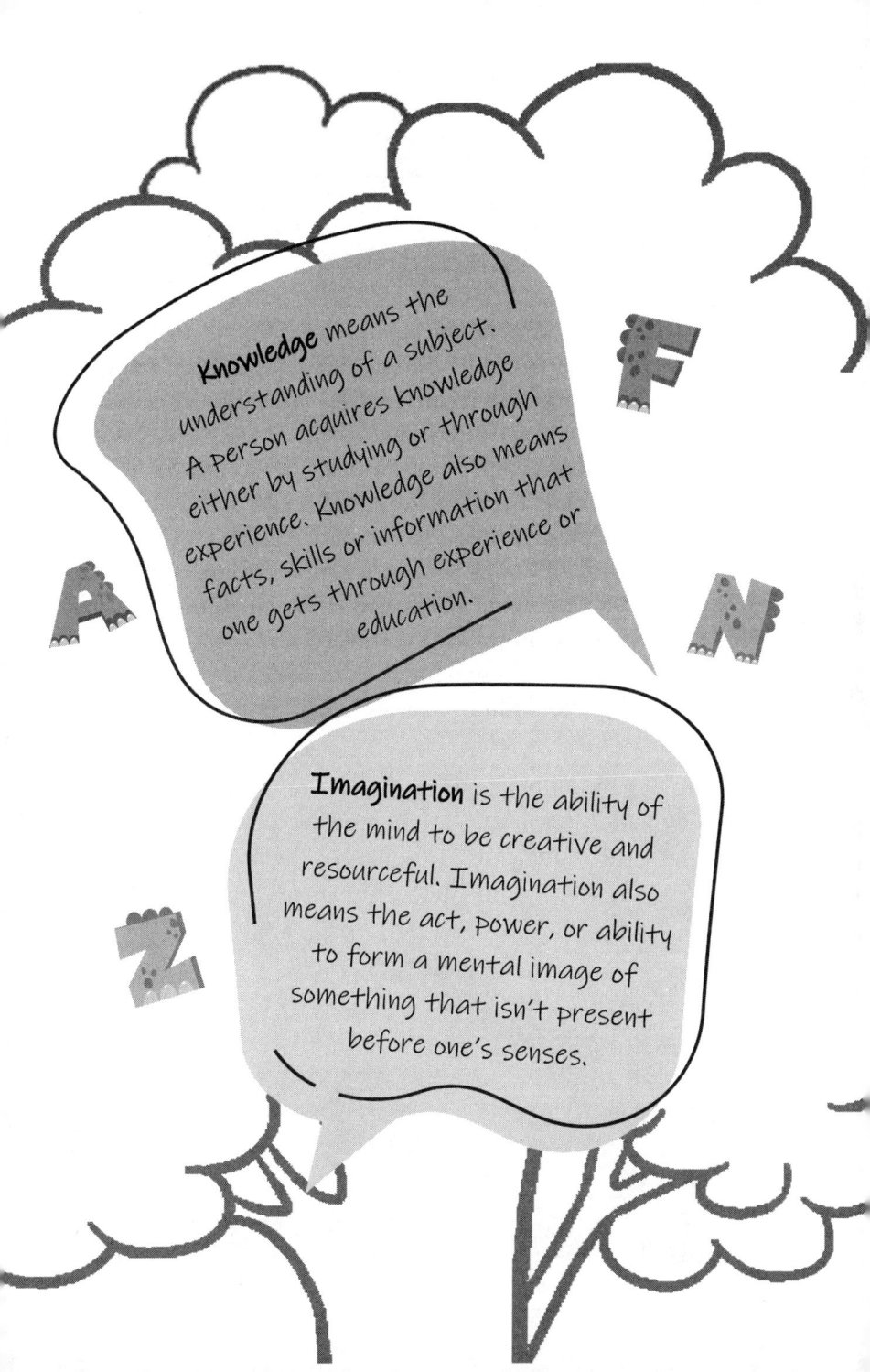

Word Games

1. Write seven sentences using the word 'book', or it can be any other word like jungle, school, food, or crow. The word has to be selected before starting the game.

   For example,
   - Yesterday, I read a wonderful book.
   - Books are a child's best friends.
   - Through books, we can travel to different places.
   - I love receiving books as birthday presents.
   - Someday in the future, I want to write a book.
   - Lucky are those who work in bookshops.
   - My school library has a vast collection of books.

2. Using your imagination, write a ten-line paragraph on a monster. It can be any monster – the monster of dirt, the monster of untidiness or the monster under your bed. Let your imagination soar. Enjoy creating a unique monster with your vivid imagination.

4
The Dwarves of Punctuation

A WEEK HAD passed since Mama had told them the stories about the letters. Having completed their homework, Aman, Rakhee and Roshni were now free. As it was raining heavily, playing outdoors was out of the question. The triplets preferred their weekends to be sunny so that they could play in the garden. They stood on the threshold of their father's study, watching their mother browse their shop's website to add catchy titles for the products in the online store. Whenever she was missing their father a lot, Mama would retreat into his study and work on his desktop computer. Mama was a superwoman; she taught in the school, looked after the shop, supervised their homework and also made special dishes for them when their cook was on leave. She even chalked out some time for her yoga and meditation. She was an efficient time manager.

'Mama, what happened after the Tree of Knowledge grew in Vocabulary Villa?' Rakhee asked.

The siblings made themselves comfortable on the carpet in the study. Their parents had purchased it during a trip to Kashmir.

'A few weeks after the Tree of Knowledge sprouted in the garden of Vocabulary Villa, Lady Language's sister

Lady Grammar appeared at the gate with her dozen odd children – the Dwarves of Punctuation,' Mama said. 'Lady Grammar too was a kind-hearted and warm person, always neatly dressed in simple gowns, but sadly her children didn't take after her.'

'Who were her children?' Roshni asked.

'They were Mr Full Stop, Miss Comma, Mr Question Mark, Miss Exclamation Mark, Miss Semicolon, Mr Colon and many others,' Mama replied. 'These Dwarves of Punctuation had a distinct personality and they were also very moody. The male dwarves had V-shaped beards, sharp noses, pointed chins and long scraggy hair. The female dwarves too had similar features and long bushy hair.'

'But, with so many people, didn't Vocabulary Villa become cramped?' Aman asked. When his cousins visited their house during the summer vacation, their house was swamped with guests and moving around became difficult.

'No,' Mama said. 'That was the magic of Vocabulary Villa. As more and more people arrived, it magically expanded itself. Every day a new wing of the house would appear.'

'Wish I could say the same for our house,' Aman sighed. 'Then I wouldn't have to share my room with my cousins Manav and Yuvi.'

'Did the dwarves play with their cousins, the letters?' Roshni asked.

'No, the Dwarves of Punctuation were very arrogant,' Mama replied. 'They seldom came out of their wing of the house, even though their mother often urged them to play with their cousins.'

'Then what happened?' asked Aman, who didn't enjoy sharing his room with his cousin brothers as they were messy, leaving their wet towels and clothes all around. But they played wonderful games with him. They also entertained him with jokes. No wonder he liked them a lot.

'Lady Grammar was getting tired of her children's arrogance. She knew that her children, though much smaller than the letters, were magical too. Lady Grammar wanted to show the world that her children too could create magic,' Mama had a mischievous smile on her face. 'One day, while the letters were playing the Game of Sentences, the game stretched on and on with no end in sight. The letters had become tired and the game wasn't making sense. Mr Full Stop, who loved wearing purple robes, watched them from the room, his tortoise-shell glasses slipping halfway down his nose. Eager to play, he joined them.'

'The moment he arrived in the garden, the Game of Sentences stopped. The tired letters were thrilled. They realised that with Mr Full Stop's entry, the Game of Sentences made sense. After taking some rest, they continued playing. Once again, when they became dizzy, Mr Full Stop put a halt to the sentence game with his presence. Like them, he was also magical and could clone himself with a shake of his head. The thrilled letters asked him to stand nearby so that he could end the game and give it a new meaning. Mr Full Stop enjoyed his role of Game Stopper,' Mama continued.

The children nodded. A single thought raced in their mind. Without the full stop, sentences would be constantly flowing. This small punctuation mark was an important one.

'Watching Mr Full Stop, his younger sister Miss Comma couldn't stop herself from jumping into the game. She wore a black gown, a red hair band on her head and red shoes on her feet. Unlike her brother, whenever Miss

Comma entered the game, she ended up separating two words, phrases or clauses in a sentence. The letters enjoyed Miss Comma's entry as they got some breathing space. After that brief period of rest, they regained the energy to continue their Game of Sentences with the next phrase in that sentence,' Mama said.

The children tried to visualise the colourfully dressed dwarves. Aman decided to draw them later.

'In a few days, Mr Question Mark, growing tired of sitting in the room, decided to play with the letters. He loved wearing funky caps and bright coloured tee shirts over shorts. But whenever he played, the letters went into doubt. They kept questioning everything. After many weeks, Miss Exclamation Mark too shed her arrogance and joined the boisterous games. She was fond of accessories; colourful bangles adorned her wrists and hoops dangled from her pointed ears. Her clothes though were always brown. But she easily got excited and constantly expressed her feelings loudly, disturbing everyone. The letters tried to avoid including Mr Question Mark and Miss Exclamation in their games, but they loved it whenever Miss Comma and Mr Full Stop played with them,' Mama sipped water from her steel water bottle.

'I hate to be left out of games when my friends are playing,' Aman said. Last week, his friends had excluded him from their game of Cricket after he had accidentally knocked the stumps with his bat, making his team lose the match.

'One day, another dwarf, Miss Semicolon, started playing with them. She had a strong personality; she wore a blue dress and pink ballerina shoes. She also loved dividing things. When she joined the Game of Sentences, she ended up separating the letters into two teams and each team by

itself made sense,' Mama had finished drinking all the water in her bottle. Making a face, she shook her empty bottle.

'Oh!' Aman said. 'I'll get you some more water from the kitchen, Mama. Please don't continue the story until I return.'

Mama opened a couple of windows. A gentle breeze wafted into the room. Within a few minutes, Aman entered the study, carrying Mama's bottle and another bottle of water and also a packet of cookies for his siblings and himself.

'Because of her strong personality, Miss Semicolon ended up pushing Miss Comma out of the game,' Mama said. She took one cookie from the packet. 'No dropping the crumbs,' she warned.

The children nodded.

'Didn't Miss Comma mind?' Rakhee asked. She popped the entire cookie into her mouth.

'No, in fact, Miss Comma was quite cool about being left out of the game,' Mama replied, frowning at the way her daughter was eating. 'She enjoyed the break and sat under the Tree of Knowledge watching them.'

'Slowly Mr Colon joined the games. He was a stuffy man with a love for pinstriped suits in different colours and black shoes. He was also very fond of making lists,' Mama laughed delightedly. 'Every time he played, there would be long lists in the game.'

'Like?' Rakhee asked. She had seen her mother's frown and dare not repeat the same mistake again. She held her second cookie in her hand, biting into it daintily.

Mama nodded approvingly. Their mother was a stickler for good manners.

'The letters were playing the Game of Sentences. They had made a sentence, DAYS OF THE WEEK,' Mama said and started writing in her notepad.

Lifting her writing pad, she showed them what she had written. 'When Mr Colon joined them, the sentence became Days of the Week: Sunday, Monday, Tuesday, Wednesday, Thursday, Friday and Saturday.'

'I like Mr Colon,' Rakhee grinned. 'I love lists.' She was always making 'to-do lists'. Sadly, she could never complete all the things on her list.

'Soon people started picking their favourite Dwarf of Punctuation,' Mama said. 'Over the course of the next few weeks, the other Dwarves of Punctuation like Miss Quotation Marks, Mr Dash, Mr Brackets, Miss Apostrophe and Miss Ellipsis too shed their timidity and started playing with the letters.'

'The Elves of Letters of the Alphabet and the Dwarves of Punctuation playing together. It must have been magical,' Aman sighed.

'Yes, that's the beauty of the language,' Mama had a distant look on her face. 'If one uses the letters imaginatively and the punctuation correctly, one can create magic with their words and language. Soon the cousins all became good friends. Within a few days, the Letters of the Alphabet and the Dwarves of Punctuation played their first Game of Stories.'

'Thank you, Mama, for such a wonderful story,' Rakhee said.

Searching the carpet for stray crumbs, she stood up. As she made her way to the door, her siblings trailed her. The children left the room, closing the door softly behind them.

> **Grammar** means the rules of a language, governing the sounds, words, sentences and other elements and also the combination of these elements and their interpretation.

Colon: It is used to give emphasis, present dialogue and introduce lists or text.

Full Stop: Is used at the end of a sentence to indicate that there is nothing more to be said on that topic.

Exclamation mark: It is usually used to indicate strong feelings or show emphasis.

Comma: Is used to separate two words, phrases or clauses in a sentence.

Semicolon: It indicates a pause typically between two main clauses, a pause more pronounced than the one indicated by a comma.

Question mark: It is used to indicate that a sentence is a question.

Punctuation refers to the symbols or marks, such as the full stop, comma, semicolon, colon, question mark, brackets and so on. Punctuation marks are used in writing to divide the written words into sentences and clauses.

Word Games

1. Look out of your window and write ten sentences about the view. You can describe what you see – the birds flying in the sky, the crow on the roof, a monkey on a tree, the clothes drying on the balcony or the terrace.

2. Describe the different sounds you can hear – the stray dogs on the road, the noise of traffic, the chirping of birds.

3. Don't forget to describe what you smell and how you feel. Bring the entire scene to life with your descriptions.

5
A Trip to the Zoo

IT HAD RAINED the entire week. Luckily, the rain stopped by Saturday night. When the children woke up on Sunday, a merry sun smiled down at them from the clear blue sky.

At breakfast, Mama told them that she would be taking them to the zoo. The excited children gobbled up their breakfast in a record time of ten minutes and were ready in fifteen. Aman and Rakhee wore identical grey shorts and blue tee shirts while Roshni wore a pink jumpsuit. Colourful caps adorned their heads.

Giving her smartly dressed children an approving look, Mama led them to the garage where the family's white car sat proudly. Mama ensured that the gardener washed it twice a week. Not a speck of dust or dirt was visible on it. Roshni sat in the passenger seat, while Aman and Rakhee made themselves comfortable in the back seat.

'Wear your seat belts,' their mother instructed.

The children strapped the seat belts around their body. Mama had told them that seat belts protected them in case of an accident.

'Let's hit the road,' Mama said. She turned the key in the ignition and started the car.

Mama was a careful driver. She navigated the vehicle safely out of their small street and now they were cruising on the main road.

'But I thought we would be driving over the roads,' Roshni looked puzzled.

'Hit the road doesn't mean we will be hitting the road, it means to start a journey or to depart, it's a figure of speech,' Mama said, stopping the car at the signal. As the light turned green, she went past a school.

Mama drove at a steady pace, keeping to her lane. They had left the city roads and were now speeding on the highway leading to the zoo.

'Understood,' the children nodded.

'Today, I'm going to kill two birds with one stone,' Mama said, as their car approached the zoo's entrance.

Above the zoo gates, was a long wooden arch, with several animals painted on it. Aman and Roshni peeped out of the windows to count the number of animals on the board.

'We are going to kill birds?' Rakhee looked scared. She was fond of birds and hated to see them in cages. If she had her way, she would have freed all the birds in captivity.

'It means I'm going to accomplish two different tasks at the same time,' Mama explained, bringing the car to a halt. She reversed the vehicle in the visitor's parking space.

'This is so confusing,' Aman scratched his head in puzzlement. 'You say one thing and it means another.'

They all got out of the car and looked around. The zoo wore signs of last week's rainfall. Drops of moisture clung to the leaves, and the damp grass rippled in the breeze. The trees looked green and were bursting with life. Several birds chirped from the trees, as though they were welcoming the visitors to the zoo.

'If we don't hurry, we will miss the boat,' Mama said, pointing to the queue of people waiting to buy entry tickets.

'Is there a lake in the zoo?' Aman asked. 'Are we going boating?'

'Missing the boat means we will miss our chance,' Mama replied. She again pointed to the queue.

'Got it,' Roshni sighed with relief. Travelling in boats made her uneasy, her food somersaulted in her stomach whenever she was on water. Fortunately, swimming didn't have that effect on her.

They joined the long line to buy the tickets. Luckily, it moved fast. Finally, it was their turn. Mama paid the money and they drifted away from the ticket window.

'Getting the tickets was a piece of cake,' Mama waved the four yellow tickets in her hand. Her eyes shone with excitement.

'I think it means easy,' Roshni said. 'Am I right, Mama?'

'Yes,' she replied, leading them to the entrance of the zoo.

The children stopped to buy packets of popcorn and chips. Before leaving home, Mama had given them strict instructions about littering public spaces and throwing food into the cages.

'The tickets cost an arm and a leg,' Mama grimaced.

'But you paid with money?' Rakhee frowned.

'It means the tickets cost Mama a lot of money,' Roshni answered.

'When something costs an arm and a leg, it doesn't literally mean cutting one's arm and leg to pay for it. It's another way of saying it's expensive or costly,' Mama explained.

'For a moment I thought Mama had to pay with her arm and leg,' Rakhee looked relieved that her mother's limbs were intact.

Mama laughed. She was in a jolly mood today. They strolled down the cobbled path, surrounded by small flowering plants on both sides. All the buds had blossomed into flowers. Butterflies flitted over the colourful flowers. A gentle breeze moved around lazily. A few clouds drifted in the sky.

They arrived outside the tiger's cage. A small board displayed its name and characteristics.

They had munched through their packet of potato chips and were now devouring the popcorn.

'The tiger has hit the sack,' Mama said, pointing to the animal sleeping in the corner.

'It means the tiger has gone to bed, right Mama?' Rakhee asked.

Mama nodded. 'We are going to have a blast today,' she winked.

The children looked at each other, confused about their mother's words. A smile lit Aman's normally serious face.

'I think to have a blast means to have a good time or to enjoy oneself,' he said.

'You nailed it,' Mama said, her eyes twinkling.

'Nailed it means he or she got it right or did it right, isn't it?' Rakhee asked.

'Yes,' Mama replied. They had stopped outside the cage with three deer. One of the zoo staff was inside, feeding the animals.

'Most people think that life for animals in the zoo is a bed of roses, unlike the animals in the wild who have to hunt for their food and end up falling prey to predators while hunting,' Mama said. 'But if you were to ask me, I think animals must hate being trapped inside cages, with people peering at them.'

'By bed of roses, you mean an easy and comfortable life or situation, right Mama?' Aman asked.

'Yes,' Mama said, turning around. She started walking down the path.

'Mama, are we going to America during our school vacation?' Roshni asked, as they trailed their mother. She stopped before a yellow flower on which a blue-green butterfly perched. The butterfly quickly flew away.

'The plan is up in the air for now,' their mother replied.

Both Rakhee and Aman looked up, while Roshni and Mama laughed.

'When I said the plan is up in the air, I meant our holiday plans are uncertain, your father and I are still thinking about it,' Mama explained. 'When something is up in the air, it means that it is still undecided or unsure.'

'Oh...' Rakhee said, her brow furrowed.. 'Sometimes you talk in such a confusing way that it's difficult to understand you.'

'Mama is playing the idiom game with us,' Roshni turned to her siblings. 'Our holiday plan is undecided because Mama and Papa are yet to see eye to eye on it,' she said.

'My girl is smart,' Mama said with a grin. 'When Roshni said that your Papa and I are yet to see eye to eye, she meant that your Papa and I are yet to agree on it.'

'Ok,' Rakhee said. 'For a moment I thought you and Papa will be looking at the atlas together,' she laughed.

'What are idioms?' Aman asked.

'Idioms are phrases or a group of words that have a meaning that is different from the individual words in it,' Mama explained.

The children nodded.

'The meaning of an idiom is different from what the words in it convey, right?' Aman asked.

'Right,' Mama said, heading towards the biggest cage.

They stood before the lion's cage. Seeing them, the animal roared, but it was not the mighty sound of the king of the jungle, rather it was a feeble one. The lion looked tired. Moving towards the corner, he lay down, resting his head on his paws.

'The lion is feeling under the weather,' Mama said. 'Before you three get more confused, it means the lion isn't feeling well.'

'I think we should call it a day,' the girls said together. 'We are tired Mama,'

'My smart children,' Mama said. 'So, you all want to quit this trip and go home?'

'Yes,' they replied, walking towards the bench to rest their tired legs.

Sitting on the cement bench, the triplets stared around, soaking in the atmosphere. A group of children led by their teacher walked past them, chatting excitedly. In the distance, an elephant trumpeted. A crow cawed from the tree.

An **idiom** is a phrase that, when taken as a whole, has a meaning one wouldn't be able to deduce from the meaning of its individual words. For example, the idiom 'pull someone's leg' means 'to play a practical joke'.

Word Games

1. Write down ten **idioms**.
2. Use the above idioms in ten different sentences.
3. Alternatively, write a hundred or a two-hundred-word essay/story using an idiom as a prompt. For example, 'To kill two birds with one stone'. Now write a story/essay starting with that idiom.
4. If you are feeling extra adventurous, you can end the story with an idiom. But choose the idiom before you start writing the story.

6
Learning to be Chefs

MAMA WAS IN the kitchen flipping through her recipe book for her favourite chocolate cake recipe. When their mother wasn't grading assignments, she would either be baking goodies for her always-hungry children or updating the shop's website.

The house was silent as Aman, Rakhee and Roshni were sitting at the small dining table reading their books.

'Can my children help me bake a chocolate cake?' Mama asked from the kitchen.

'Yeah,' they replied. Leaving their books, they ran towards their mother.

Their mother was in her favourite brown slacks and black shirt. She wore a purple apron over her clothes. Mama was always neat and tidy and her kitchen was spotlessly clean with not a single spoon out of place or the tiniest speck of dirt visible on the counter.

'Wash your hands first,' she instructed. She watched them scrub their hands at the kitchen sink. One by one, they wiped their hands with the kitchen towel.

'I'll combine cooking with a game,' Mama said, with a twinkle in her eyes.

'That will be super,' the children said. They were always ready for games.

'Will we be playing in teams?' Aman asked. He always preferred to be in Mama's team as that would ensure a victory in any game.

'No,' Mama said. 'Each one of you will be playing for yourself.'

'Hope it's not a difficult game?' Roshni asked.

'It's easy,' Mama replied. 'When I ask you something, tell me what it resembles?'

'Understood,' Aman and Roshni said together. Rakhee just nodded.

'Let's start,' Mama said excitedly. Picking up a pair of blue gloves, she inserted her hands inside them. Waving her hands, she asked, 'I'm wearing gloves as blue as the...'

'Summer sky,' the three children said together.

Mama arranged the ingredients for the cake on the kitchen counter.

'Break this slab of sweet chocolate into small pieces in a bowl,' she instructed Roshni and Rakhee.

The girls broke the slab of chocolate; soon the bowl was filled with small pieces.

Mama placed the bowl into the microwave and set the timer.

Beep. Beep. Beep.

Mama removed the bowl of melted chocolate from the microwave.

'I've chocolate as dark and velvety as the...,' she stirred the melted chocolate with a spoon.

'Night sky,' Aman said.

'The chocolate is as smooth as...?' she looked at Rakhee and Roshni.

'Silk,' they replied.

Mama removed the brick of butter from the fridge and cut a slice from it.

'Into the melted chocolate, I'll add butter as pale as…,' Mama sang while chopping butter into small cubes.

The girls giggled.

'Early morning sunshine,' Roshni said.

'Blend the butter and chocolate,' she instructed Aman.

Aman mixed the butter and chocolate with a spoon.

SPLAT.

Sticky gobs of chocolate hit the wall.

Mama frowned when she saw the chocolate stains on the wall. She disliked a dirty kitchen.

'Clean it right now, before the stains solidify,' she said.

Taking a cloth, Aman wiped the stains until the wall was back to its earlier spotless self.

'I'll add flour as white as…,' she tipped the small bowl of flour into the chocolate mix.

'Snow,' Roshni said.

'Milk,' Aman added.

'What else do I add?' Mama tapped her chin.

'Eggs that look like a zero,' Rakhee and Roshni grinned.

'Not bad,' their mother said. 'My girls know what goes into a cake and they are also learning the game fast.'

'I'll crack open the eggs for you,' Aman cracked two eggs with a butter knife, littering the kitchen with pieces of egg shells.

Mama shook her head at the mess he had made.

'I'll whip the eggs until they are light and frothy as…,' Mama whisked the eggs with an electric whisk.

'Soap bubbles,' Aman said.

'Clouds,' the girls screamed.

'What else do I need?' Mama asked, pouring the beaten eggs into the bowl of chocolate.

'Walnuts as round as a circle,' Aman sang.

'Good idea,' Mama nodded. She opened the jar of nuts. A single walnut lolled inside.
She rolled the nut between her hands.
'Add it fast, we are hungry,' Roshni urged.
Mama tapped the walnut shell with her butter knife. She hit it harder. The walnut didn't break.
'The shell is as hard…,' she moaned.
'As a stone,' Aman made a sad face.
Mama banged the walnut against the kitchen counter. Crack.
The shell split into two. She scooped out the fleshy part, and chopping it into small pieces, added it to the cake batter.
Adding half a cup of milk into the bowl, she whisked it in one direction until the liquid blended. She poured the cake batter into a greased microwave dish. Then she slid it into the microwave.
The excited children peered through the glass door of the microwave, watching the cake rise.
'The cake looks as soft and fluffy as…,' Mama said.
'Cotton candy,' Aman said.
'A feather,' the girls answered.
'Why is my kitchen as dirty as a…,' she asked, looking at the chocolate splattered on the counter and the pieces of shells littering the ground.
'Pigsty,' the three children said together.
'So, what do we do now?' Mama questioned.
'We will clean the kitchen while the cake is getting baked,' Rakhee said. Aman picked up a broom and swept the kitchen. Rakhee mopped the floor while Roshni wiped the stains from the kitchen counter.

BECOME A GRAMMAR GURU

'The game we played was the Game of Similes,' Mama explained. 'A simile is a word or a phrase that compares one thing to another by using the words "like" or "as".'

'It was super fun,' Roshni grinned.

'We enjoyed playing this game,' Rakhee said.

'Can I also make one simile?' Aman asked.

Mama nodded.

'Similes are as fun as…,' he smiled.

'Games,' Mama and the girls replied together.

A **simile** is an expression we use when comparing two things using the words 'like' or 'as'.

Soon the delicious smell of cake filled the kitchen. The children stared at the microwave as though hoping the cake would walk towards them.

'Thank you for helping me. Now the kitchen is as clean as a...,' Mama said.

'Whistle,' the three children said together.

'And my children are as good as...,' Mama hugged her children.

'Gold,' Aman laughed.

Mama removed the cake from the microwave and placed it on the counter to cool.

'Can I take a photo of the cake to send to Dad?' Rakhee asked.

Mama handed her the mobile phone and watched her daughter click a few pictures.

A little later, Mama cut thick slices of the gooey chocolate cake for all of them. The melt-in-the-mouth cake was the best one they had in a long time. It was all the more special as they had all helped their mother make it.

BECOME A GRAMMAR GURU

Word Games

1. Write a short essay on summer, monsoon or a cloudy day, using similes in a creative way.
2. Describe your dream or nightmare with the help of similes.
3. Solve a mystery with just one clue, that is a simile. For example, Someone broke into your neighbour's house and stole many expensive items. All you have as a clue is a simile, 'as slow as a snail'. Write the story and solve the mystery.

7
Homing in on Homophones

THE CHILDREN HAD finished playing in the garden and returned to the house for water; their throats were parched as it was a hot day and all the running around had tired them. They decided to ask their mother if she wanted anything or any help.

Aman, Roshni and Rakhee stood at the threshold of their parents' bedroom, watching their Mama. She was sitting on the bed and grading the answer sheets with a frown on her face. In school, the students constantly approached Mama for extra help and she never turned anyone down. Her classes were always fun and she was a lenient teacher. But she was very particular about spelling and grammar. She also disliked badly written assignments.

'Mama looks irritated,' Rakhee whispered to her siblings.

'I'm sure the students have messed up their assignments,' Roshni replied.

'Mama, are you angry about something?' Aman asked.

'Yes,' she said. 'When my grade six students *write* their essays, they never ensure they have the *right* spellings. I'm always at *sea* when I *see* their assignments,' Mama said tiredly. There were dark circles around her eyes. Mama always looked exhausted after the exams as she had to grade hundreds of answer sheets. The children helped as much as they could with household chores, but Mama ensured that she did most of the work. Rakhee felt sad for her mother.

'Come *here* and *hear* my woes,' Mama beckoned her children. 'But don't be bad by wearing your muddy shoes when you sit on my bed.'

Aman stepped into the room. Rakhee and Roshni did the same. This would be an interesting game.

'This sounds like fun,' Aman said. Removing their shoes, they sat around their mother on the bed.

'Did the balm you apply on your *heel, heal* your pain?' Rakhee asked, touching her mother's right foot.

'It's much better now,' Mama replied. 'And now that my angel has touched my *heel*, it will *heal* faster,' she ruffled her daughter's hair.

'I'm thinking about *whether* I should wear my jacket when I go out to my friend's house because the *weather* looks like it's going to rain,' Aman said.

'Take it just in case,' Mama suggested. Turning to Roshni, she said, 'Your turn now.'

'I was reading a book about a brave *knight* who saved people at *night*,' Roshni said, making her eyes big and dropping her voice to a whisper.

'My drama queen,' Mama pulled her close in a hug. Roshni buried her face into her mother's shoulder.

'I'm going to write a *tale* about a cat's *tail* for my school assignment,' Aman announced.

'Diamonds are sold in *carats* while *carrots* are sold in kilograms,' Rakhee added. She had just read about diamonds in the newspaper. She was surprised to learn that diamonds were sold in carats.

'When you *two* go out to play again, I *too* will join you, as I have completed my homework,' Roshni added.

'I've decided that *except* for cash I'll not *accept* any other gift this birthday,' Aman winked.

'Someone is hinting big time,' Mama rolled her eyes. Aman always dropped hints before his birthday about the gifts he wanted. Sadly, no one paid attention to his words.

'A change in the weather *affects* our health, but sadly these changes in the climate are the *effect* of man's destruction of natural resources,' Roshni said.

Everyone turned to stare at Roshni. They were all aware that she had started helping in their school's Climate Warrior's Club. She had helped her seniors paint posters on climate change.

'I hate to sit *idle;* my inspiration comes from my eighty-year-old hardworking grandmother who is my *idol*,' Mama said. 'In fact, my grandmother taught the entire village about the benefits of hard work.'

The children had met their great-grandmother a couple of times. She was a tough woman, always running around her house, cooking, looking after the animals, gardening, and serving food to her innumerable guests.

'I do *not* know how to make the *knot* of a tie,' Aman said. 'That's why I usually ask Dad to do it for me.'

Among the three children, Aman's tie was the worst. It had all kinds of stains, as Aman always managed to drop whatever he was eating on his tie. The girls never touched it as they were worried about their hygiene.

'You must *know* that to say *no* is not always a bad thing,' Roshni said. 'Sometimes it works in our favour.'

She had seen a book titled *The Art of Saying No* on her father's bookshelf in his study.

'That man was jailed because he was caught stealing steel trunks,' Aman pointed to an article in the newspaper. 'Moral of the story: Never *steal steel* trunks,' he said.

Everyone laughed. They had all read about the burglar who loved steel trunks and how he was caught. It had made headlines for a couple of days.

'You are so funny,' Roshni laughed.

'I've always wanted to live in a house by the beach. Sadly, we can't *see* the *sea* from our house,' Rakhee said.

'There is no sea in Bengaluru,' Aman pointed out. 'So how can you *see* the *sea* from our house?'

'That was just an example, dumbo,' his sister hit him with a pillow.

Before a full-fledged pillow fight started, Mama said, 'Let me tell you a story. Once upon a time, there was a king who had just one *son*, who was the *sun* of his universe. Being the only child, he was the rightful *heir* to the kingdom; he loved riding his horse enjoying the fresh morning *air*. The prince had many pets, but his favourite was a cat with a long *tail*, and he loved telling the cat a tall *tale* every night,' Mama said.

'What a sweet and funny story,' Roshni giggled. She tried to visualise the prince telling his cat tall tales.

'I read somewhere that if we eat hair *dye*, we may *die*,' Aman said, making a sad face.

'Who eats hair dye?' Mama frowned.

'Only gluttons like you will think of eating hair dye,' Rakhee said.

Mama shook her head. Sometimes her children ended up fighting for the silliest reasons. She stared at Aman. She was expecting him to argue, but his forehead was creased in a frown. Either he hadn't heard his sister, or perhaps he had decided to ignore her comment.

'Okay, here is another one,' Aman said. 'A good *sole* in shoes makes for a happy *soul*.'

'Really pathetic,' Rakhee grimaced. 'I would have marked you two out of ten.'

Aman flung the pillow at his sister. Expertly dodging it, she caught it and flung it back at him.

'Let me tell you a story about a *knight* who used to roam the streets at *night*. One day, the knight came across a silver *hare*; he was so enchanted with its colour, that he wanted a *hair* from its tail,' Mama said.

'Lovely,' the children clapped.

'Your answers are the best, Mama,' Rakhee said.

'Which one of you will buy the *flour* for me from the supermarket, so that I can make a *flower*-shaped cake for all of you today?' Mama asked.

'Me,' Aman said

'All of us,' the girls added.

'Is Mama planning to bake a cake for us?' Aman asked his sisters in a whisper.

'I heard you,' their mother arched her eyebrows. 'Will bake for you after a few days. First tell me, are you enjoying playing the HPG?' her eyes twinkled.

'HPG?' Aman looked puzzled.

'What is HPG?' Rakhee frowned.

'The Homophone Game,' Mama laughed. 'You all played the game like professionals. No one can say it was the first time you were playing the HP Game.'

'We are the HP experts,' Aman said.

The girls tossed their heads, bursting into boisterous laughter.

Roshni left the room, followed by Aman. They returned carrying small glasses of water and salted biscuits for everyone.

'My children are growing up so fast,' Mama sighed, sipping her water gratefully.

The children stood at the window watching a squirrel scamper up a tree.

Homophones are two or more words which have the same pronunciation or sound, but different spelling and meanings. For example, rice and rise, mail and male, pale and pail, hail and hale, sail and sale, team and teem, meet and meat.

Word Games

1. Make a list of homophones.
2. Describe your first day in school, a walk in the park or a favourite relative, using the homophones from your list.
3. Write a story with a character who mixes up her words.

8
Howzat Homonyms

THE HOUSE WAS quiet as Aman, Rakhee and Roshni completed their English assignments. Whenever the triplets did their homework, the usually noisy house turned silent. They were sitting at the dining table. Mama was also sitting with them; she was making lesson plans for her students. Each one of them had a look of concentration on their face as their hands raced over their notebook, filling it with neat rows of handwriting. Their mother always stressed the importance of writing neatly and proofreading their assignments so there were no errors.

'At last!' Roshni said, closing her notebook. 'I finally completed my English assignment.'

'Me too,' Aman sighed. 'Now I can play cricket with the boys from the next building.'

'Whew, this was a tough one!' Rakhee sighed. 'I was dreading it, but thanks to the motivation from you two, I finished it super fast. Now I can read the book I borrowed from the library.'

'What's up, my babies?' Mama raised questioning eyes at her children.

Aman whispered to his sisters. The conversation turned frantic as their mother watched with an amused look on her face.

'We will play a game with you, Mama,' Aman grinned. 'Each one of us will read out our assignments to you,' Rakhee said, 'and you have to mark us on it.'

'Done,' Mama said, sitting up straight.

Like her children, Mama too loved playing games. Many times, she joined them in the garden for football or badminton. If the game involved some aspect of grammar, she loved it even more.

'I'll go first,' Roshni lifted her notebook and started reading. 'Yesterday, as part of my welfare work in school, I visited the neighbourhood slum. I was sitting in the biggest room in the Community Centre; though the room wasn't *bright*, the children were very *bright*. They not only answered all my questions quickly, they also asked me intelligent questions. As I passed the cakes and cookies sponsored by the welfare *arm* of the Cellme company, I saw a student waving his *arm* to get my attention. I had forgotten to serve him his snacks. After serving him, I left for my school. When I reached school, I realised I had lost the *band* I wear around my wrist. I remember fidgeting with it while the school *band* was playing my favourite tune.'

'Not bad,' Mama said. 'Eight out of ten,' she made the gesture of a tick.

'Me next,' Rakhee jumped up and down in her chair. 'In the afternoon, when I was sleeping, I heard the neighbour's dog *bark* while he was being taken for his usual stroll around their house. Looking out of the window, I couldn't stop laughing when I saw that someone had stuck a poster of a cat on the *bark* of the mango tree. As I watched, someone from the road hurled a rock over the wall. The sound of the *rock* falling was drowned out when another neighbour played loud *rock* music. As I turned around to return to my bed, the old grandmother in the house opposite picked up her shears and slowly *rose* from the ground as she had finished pruning the *rose* plant.'

'Super,' Mama smiled. 'Nine out of ten.'

'Yippee,' Rakhee pumped her fist in the air.

Roshni made a sad face.

'You are next,' Mama turned to Aman.

'I don't think I can compete with my two genius sisters,' he stuck out his tongue.

'Today I had to *address* a group of students in another school, but my teacher didn't give me the school's *address*. However, I reached the *right* place after taking a few *right* turns. But, while returning to school, I got lost. I realised I had taken a *circular* route when I saw the same person again, standing on the street corner, handing out a *circular*.'

'Hmm... can improve it,' Mama pursed her lips. 'Seven and a half out of ten.'

'Over the weekend, we will try to polish it so that you give us also a nine out of ten,' Roshni and Aman said.

'Copycats,' Rakhee smirked.

'That's the spirit,' Mama said as she high-fived Aman and Roshni.

'Now it's our turn to grade you,' Rakhee giggled.

'By the way, Mama, how is your headache now?' Aman asked with a concerned expression on his face.

The children were worried as last night their mother had gone to bed early complaining of a headache.

'I am *well,* thank you. Unlike my grandmother who had to draw water for her bath from the *well,* I just have to open the tap in the morning. My grandmother was a *tender* person, who would never *tender* the exact change when she was sent on an errand by her mother. Once she got distracted by a boy playing with his *bat* under a tree where a *bat* hung upside down from one of the branches,' Mama said.

'Ten out of ten,' the triplets chorused, exchanging amused looks.

'Thank you, my lovely teachers,' Mama said with a straight face.

'You are our most favourite student,' Rakhee giggled.

'I try to do my best, teacher,' Mama said playfully.

'Can we call this game Howzat Homonyms?' Aman asked.

'How about H2?' Roshni asked.

'Howzat Homonyms is better,' Rakhee said.

'Both titles are super,' Mama added. 'But you must promise me that on rainy days when you can't play outdoors, you will teach the children of our neighbourhood this game.'

'Done deal,' they promised.

'In fact, we are planning to message Dad using homonyms. Can I have your mobile phone?' Roshni asked.

'That's a super idea,' Mama smiled, handing her mobile phone to Roshni.

The children huddled together as Roshni clicked a selfie. Then she typed a message to their father.

A **Homonym** is when two words have the same spelling and pronunciation, but **differ in meaning.** For example, They saw a big bear. Here bear is an animal. The doctor said that the patient must bear the pain for twenty-four hours. Here bear refers to tolerating or putting up with the pain.

Word Games

1. Using a set of homonyms, write a short essay on your favourite birthday, food, outfit or your favourite place in the house.
2. Describe a relaxed Sunday using homonyms.
3. Write a two-hundred-word essay about yourself using homonyms.

9
It's Raining Metaphors

AMAN AND RAKHEE were lying in bed, nursing a cold and a fever, while the third triplet, Roshni, was bent over her homework notebook, completing her assignment.

Their mother was correcting her tenth-grade assignments. Besides school work, she had piles of sheets to read, as whenever her students wrote anything, they would plead with her to go over it.

'What did you learn in school today?' Rakhee croaked.

'We learnt about metaphors,' Roshni replied.

'I wish I hadn't fallen sick,' Aman said, sipping his herbal tea to soothe his throat.

'Today, I'll be your teacher,' Roshni announced. 'I'll teach you about metaphors.' Lifting her notebook, she read from it. 'A metaphor is a figure of speech that gets together or pairs the intangible with the literal. I'll simplify it further. A metaphor is a comparison between two things that are unrelated. Like when I say, you two are drowning in a sea of sickness. In this case, the intangible is the sea which we can't see and the literal is the sickness that you two have. So, when I say that you both are drowning in a sea of sickness, I am just trying to convey more forcefully what you are actually undergoing.'

'I got it,' Rakhee nodded. 'With a metaphor, you are conveying a thought, else you could have made an ordinary statement like, "You two are sick".'

'Though my head feels woozy, I also understood that even though metaphors are exaggerations, they actually paint a very clear image,' Aman said. Steam curled out from the cup he was holding. 'Metaphors have more impact than ordinary statements.'

'You two are fast learners,' Roshni smiled. 'Or maybe I am a great teacher,' she lifted the collar of the green shirt-dress she was wearing. 'Or maybe the cold and cough has actually cleared the cobwebs from your brain,' she winked.

'Stop fishing for compliments,' Aman scowled.

'Mr Grumpy, do you realise that you just used a metaphor?' Roshni arched her eyebrows.

Aman's eyes widened as he sipped his herbal tea.

'I'm smart,' he grinned.

'I'm sure it was a fluke,' Roshni snorted. 'Without realising it, you used a metaphor that shows one's desire for getting praise. It doesn't mean one is actually fishing, one is just talking or acting in a way so as to gather more compliments.'

'This semester, the teachers have drowned us in a sea of work,' Rakhee said, making the action of a drowning woman flailing her arms, as though asking for help.

'Good,' Roshni nodded at her sister. 'Time was a thief today while Miss Malati was teaching us metaphors.'

'When you said time was a thief today, you didn't mean that time wore a mask and dark glasses and entered the classroom to steal, you just meant that time passed quickly today. Am I right, sis?' Rakhee asked, blowing her nose into a tissue paper.

'You are spot on,' Roshni said. 'Looks like the cold and

fever is suiting you two. Normally you both would have taken some time to understand, but today you dumbos are very quick on the uptake.'

'Though Rakhee and I are feeling blue today, we actually missed school,' Aman said. 'And I need not explain to the girl who attended school today that blue in this case means sad, not that we have actually turned blue.'

'Yes, smarty-pants, I understood what you were trying to say,' Roshni rolled her eyes. 'I'm sure you two were the apples of Mama's eyes today. She must have pampered you like crazy. She took leave from school today just to take care of you both.'

'Yes, today we were extra dear to Mama, so we became the apples of her eyes,' Rakhee agreed. 'She pampered us like mad and also spent a lot of time with us.'

'By the way, did the replacement Biology teacher come today?' Aman asked.

'Yes, she came today. Her name is Renuka Mathur. She has a very bubbly personality, and the icing on the cake was that after the introduction, she gave us a free period.'

'Gosh, stop talking like that,' Aman chided. 'Instead of saying bubbly personality, can't you just say cheerful. And instead of saying the icing on the cake, can't you just say that something wonderful happened on the heels of a happy day. Now that you mention cake, go buy us cupcakes from the neighbourhood bakery,' he ordered.

'I agree with Aman, you had no business mentioning cake and icing,' Rakhee joined the conversation. 'You better get us cake now.'

Their mother entered the room with two strips of tablets. The children on the bed groaned. They knew it was time for their evening medicine.

'Fine, I'll get the cake for you two bears with sore heads,' Roshni scowled, stomping out of the room.

'What did she mean by that?' Aman and Rakhee asked their mother.

'She meant that you two are in a bad mood. It also means that you both are very irritable and also grumpy today,' Mama explained.

'It's raining cats and dogs, I just hope Roshni has taken her umbrella,' Aman said.

'Yes bro,' Roshni said, entering the room. She was carrying a brown paper bag in her hands. 'I knew it was going to rain cats and dogs, I mean rain heavily, so I was prepared. I believe that being forewarned is forearmed.'

'Here she goes again,' her siblings rolled their eyes.

There was complete silence as the children gobbled up their cupcakes and sweet buns which were still warm. Luckily Roshni had bought extra, so everyone had seconds.

A **metaphor** is a figure of speech that gets together or pairs the intangible with the literal. Metaphors are a form of figurative language which refer to words or expressions that mean something different from their literal definition. A metaphor can also be said to be an implied comparison.

Word Games

1. Go to the market and buy five metaphors. Meaning, write five metaphors about your trip to the market. Alternatively, you can write five metaphors about your visit to the doctor's clinic or a birthday party.
2. Pick up five metaphors from the library in your school. Describe your library period using a few metaphors.

10
You Said It

AMAN AND RAKHEE had recovered from their viral fever, but Mama still made them wear warm clothes. Even Roshni had been forced to put on a sweater. Mama as usual was in her favourite place, on the brown single-seater sofa, in her pink and blue kaftan. The siblings sat on the three-seater, watching their mother correct her assignments. Mama never raised her voice at her students or punished them. But now there was a harassed expression on her usually pleasant face.

'What is troubling you, Mama?' Aman asked, keeping the book he was reading on the low table in front of him.

'Are the assignments so bad?' Rakhee questioned.

'Why so sad, Mama?' Roshni looked concerned.

'Last month, I gave my students an assignment. They were supposed to write a 1200-word short story. They all have vivid imaginations, their stories have decent plots and characters. In fact, they all have written good stories, but they still need to make more effort,' Mama replied.

'What does that mean?' Roshni asked. They dreaded reaching high school as then Mama would become their English teacher. They knew their mother was a hard taskmaster and would show them no mercy or slack.

'When I say they need to make more effort, I mean just that. The decent storyline and plotting could have been enhanced with better writing. A good writing style makes even an average plot very readable. Throughout the story, they have written, he said, she said, they said, we said,' Mama sighed. 'I wish they had made an effort to use a synonym for said. That would have made the writing much better.'

'Oh,' Aman nodded in understanding. 'But in which way would a synonym for said have helped the stories?'

'A synonym for said would have enhanced the dialogue part of the story. The conversation between the characters would have had a better flow,' Mama explained. 'Usage of synonyms would have broken the monotony of seeing too many said, said, said.'

'I think I understand what you are trying to say,' Rakhee nodded. She was reading a book and had just read a few synonyms for said in the third chapter.

'Can each one of you think of different words you can use instead of said?' Mama asked.

'I can,' Aman raised his hand, as though he was still in the classroom. He leaned closer to his mother, trying to get her attention.

'My good boy,' Mama ruffled his hair.

'Instead of said, we can use *told, stated, explained, replied, answered, narrated*,' Aman said, with a large smile on his face. He was quite proud of himself for thinking of so many synonyms for said.

'Good,' Mama nodded. 'It also depends on the context. If someone is telling a story, instead of said, we can use *narrated*. If someone is replying to our question, we can say *answered* or *replied*, if someone is making us understand some facts, we can say *explained*.

BECOME A GRAMMAR GURU

'Now my turn,' Roshni said excitedly. 'Instead of said, we can say, *advised, suggested, informed, ordered, instructed, expressed* and *revealed*,' she said quickly, as though the words were in a hurry to rush out of her mouth.

'Very good,' Mama said. 'Again, it depends on the scenario. If someone is giving a command, we can use the word *ordered* or even *commanded* instead of said. If someone is telling us about something, like a change in the train timing, we can say *informed* or *notified*, if someone is elaborating something or telling us more, we can say *revealed, confided* or *disclosed*. The best thing is that said has plenty of synonyms to choose from.'

'I'd like to suggest that instead of said, we can say, *declared, uttered, murmured, muttered, whispered, advised* or *even suggested*,' Rakhee added.

'Well done girl,' Mama's eyes shone with pride. 'When someone says something loudly or firmly then *declared* would be the appropriate synonym for said. If someone speaks softly, then *whispered* would be the right word to use. If someone talks under their breath, or is speaking to himself or herself, we can say *muttered, mumbled* or *murmured*. If someone gives advice, we can say he *advised* or he *suggested*. All these synonyms enhance our writing. The purpose of a story is to make the reader live that experience and a good storyteller brings to life every part of the story in every possible way,' Mama explained.

The children listened keenly to their mother's explanation. She was a patient teacher who never got irritated with their mistakes or raised her voice even when she had to repeat something several times.

'But, it's perfectly all right to use said too. There is no compulsion on the writer to use words that are synonyms of said. Sometimes using said is better, as too many different synonyms for it may distract the reader,' she added.

'There must be many synonyms for said, right Mama?' Roshni asked.

'Yes,' Mama continued. 'Alternately, you can say, he *voiced his opinion*, she *remarked*, they *responded*, she *mouthed*, and when you want to repeat your denial, you can say, she *reiterated*, or she *repeated*.'

'Do all these synonyms really enhance our writing?' Aman asked.

'Yes,' Mama replied. 'They make the flow of the conversations much better, they break the monotony of using said. And if one were to use an action along with these dialogue tags, it would be the icing on the cake.'

'Action meaning?' Roshni frowned.

'For instance, I can say, *she whispered with a wink*; or *he sighed, lowering his head*; or *she muttered, clasping her hands*,' Mama explained.

'Cool,' Rakhee's eyes were wide. 'Can I say, *she suggested, her eyes dancing with mischief*. Does it sound nice?'

'It sounds great,' Mama said with an approving look on her face.

A **synonym** is a word that means **exactly or nearly** the same as another word in the same language. If you replace a particular word in a sentence with its synonym, the meaning of the sentence won't change. For example, She closed the window. She shut the window. Both sentences mean the same, though 'closed' was replaced with 'shut'.

BECOME A GRAMMAR GURU

'Can I say, *he mouthed with a frown on his face*, or *she said, scrunching her nose?* Are both okay?' Aman asked.

'Both show that you have a creative bent of mind,' Mama replied, 'If you work hard, your assignments will sparkle.'

'Yippee,' Aman pumped his fist in the air.

'And I will say, *he chimed in with a laugh*,' Roshni said.

Mama looked delighted. 'My children are quick learners. I'm sure when you all write your story assignments, you will do a great job and make your teacher happy, just as you have made me happy today.'

Taking out their notebooks, the children started writing whatever Mama had taught them today. It would come in handy in the future. Aman peeped into his sisters' notebooks, he was sure they would have written down everything their mother had explained.

Word Games

1. Write down a paragraph from a book. Now using synonyms rewrite that paragraph so that the meaning remains the same.
2. Make a list of twenty-five words and their synonyms. Write a short story using all these synonyms.

11

Amazing Alliterations

IT WAS A gloomy Sunday afternoon. Through their window, the triplets saw dark clouds marching with a purpose, as though they were going for a battle. Thunder rumbled and lightning constantly split the sky.

Unable to play outdoors as they usually did, Aman, Rakhee and Roshni huddled on the sofa in the living room, watching their mother browse the gift shop's website on her laptop.

A little later, she closed her laptop. Taking out vegetables from the refrigerator in the kitchen, she sat at the dining table and started cutting the veggies for dinner. Bundled in warm clothes, the children sipped their hot chocolate milk.

'Mama, we are bored. Can you join us for a game of Carrom?' Aman asked. 'You can be my partner.' He preferred being in his mother's team, as she was a really good Carrom player.

'Let me finish my work,' Mama said, peeling a carrot.

'That's a mountain of vegetables, it will take you an hour,' Rakhee groaned. 'We want to play now.'

'Can we play some other game?' Roshni asked. Carrom wasn't her favourite game.

She had finished reading the book she had borrowed from the library and now had nothing to do. Their mother had strict rules about spending time online. She preferred them to play outdoor games or read books. Some indoor games like Ludo, Scrabble, Chinese Checkers and Carrom were given the green signal by her.

'Let's play the game Amazing Alliterations,' Mama said. 'We can all play the game and I can still do my vegetables. It's a win-win situation.'

'This game of alliterations sounds difficult,' Aman made a face. 'I think Carrom will be easier. You have a valley of vegetables to cut, so we will wait until you complete your chores.'

'Wow,' Mama's eyes were wide. 'You have already started playing the game.'

'I don't understand,' Aman looked puzzled. A frown creased his forehead. 'I haven't started any game.'

'Valley of vegetables is an example of alliteration,' Mama said. 'An alliteration is a literary device in which two or more words that appear one after another have the same initial stressed consonant sound. For example, annoying ants, pretty pink, short shawl, tall tree, mad morning, lucky lady, dirty door, long lizard, silk sari, naughty nose. All these words have the same initial letters and sound.'

'But I didn't say vegetable valley, I said valley of vegetables,' Aman replied.

'Mama, what Aman said is not a perfect example of alliteration, right?' Rakhee asked.

Leaving the sofa, she walked towards the dining table to sit beside her mother. Seeing her, Aman and Roshni too joined them.

It had started raining. They watched the thick ropes of water fall to the ground.

'Hope my new plant will be safe,' Rakhee said. She had won a potted plant in school yesterday for best handwriting.

'Don't worry about it,' Mama assured her. 'I brought it in last night. It's in the kitchen now.'

'You are the best,' Rakhee gave her mother a flying kiss.

'Now back to the game,' Mama said. 'In an alliteration, all words may not begin with the same letter. So, valley of vegetables fits well into an example of an alliteration as the two words in close proximity of each other begin with the same alphabet and have the same consonant sound.'

The children started shelling the peas to help their mother. Mama was making *matar paneer*.[2] It was their most favourite dish. They would have it with hot *rotis*[3] speckled with *ghee*.[4]

'Ok,' Roshni nodded, popping a few peas into her mouth. 'So, if I say, Mental mathematics drives most people mad, will that still be an alliteration?'

'Yes,' Mama replied. 'Mental mathematics makes most men mad, would be a perfect example of an alliteration. But even your sentence can stake a claim to being called an alliteration.'

'I like this game,' Aman looked excited. 'Here is a good example of a perfect alliteration, cutting crazy carrots,' he laughed delightedly at his words.

---

2 Matar Paneer is a North Indian dish consisting of peas and paneer in a tomato-based sauce.
3 A roti is a round flatbread native to the Indian subcontinent.
4 Ghee is a type of clarified butter, originating from India.

'Boring beans,' Roshni grimaced.

She disliked beans, always picking them out from *upma*[5] and *pulao*[6] and leaving them on the edge of her plate. Taking a couple of cluster beans in her hand, she made them dance like puppets. The others watched the vegetable show with interest.

'Pretty potatoes,' Rakhee added. She loved potatoes and could eat them for breakfast, lunch and dinner.

'Potatoes aren't pretty,' Aman laughed.

'Neither are carrots crazy, they are actually good for the eyes,' she replied.

'No fighting,' Mama warned.

'But beans are indeed boring,' both said together.

They had finished shelling all the peas. They pushed the bowl towards their mother.

'Beans are good for health,' Mama said. 'My mother would make me eat them at least thrice a week.'

'The weather is worrisome,' Aman looked out of the window.

The wind whooshed through the trees. Rain pounded the ground. Aman groaned. The garden would be a slush pond tomorrow, making it difficult for them to play.

'The trees are talking,' Roshni added.

'The wind is whispering through the willows,' Rakhee said.

'Good one, Rakhee,' Mama nodded approvingly.

---

5 Upma is a thick porridge made from dry-roasted semolina or coarse rice flour, more popular in the South Indian states.

6 Pulao is a rice dish cooked with a variety of ingredients such as vegetables, meat, and spices. There are both vegetarian and non-vegetarian options available.

BECOME A GRAMMAR GURU

'My Mama is magnificent,' moving towards her mother, Rakhee hugged her.

'That's so sweet of you,' Mama said, hugging her back. 'You children are learning the game fast. The perfect example of alliteration is, Seema sells sea shells on a seashore.'

'Ponga Padam pinched a pumpkin,' Aman said loudly.

'I can't imagine Ponga Padam pinching a pumpkin,' Rakhee giggled. 'What if the pumpkin bites him?'

Everyone started laughing. The vegetables were all neatly diced into cubes. Now their mother would just need to cook the pulao in the pressure cooker and their dinner would be ready within half an hour. She would have the time to play one round of Carrom with them.

'Jealous *jalebi*[7] jiggled and jogged,' Roshni added.

'I prefer the jalebi to be inside my stomach with lots of hot *rabri*[8] instead of jogging and jiggling,' Aman grinned. 'I'm sure the jalebi will run faster than me, so I won't be able to catch it.'

'That's true,' Rakhee nodded mischievously. 'And the jalebi will get dirty if it runs on the road.'

'Then you will have to wash it before you eat it,' Roshni added.

'No,' Rakhee shook her head. 'That runaway jalebi will never see the inside of my stomach. Aman can eat it, I won't touch it.'

---

7 Jalebi is a spiral shaped crisp and juicy sweet made with all-purpose flour, gram flour and sugar syrup.
8 Rabri also known as rabdi is a North Indian traditional sweet dish made with full fat milk, sugar, cardamoms and nuts.

'As if I will eat that jalebi,' Aman scowled.

'Right now, what is running away is my children's imagination,' their mother laughed.

'Roshni and Rakhee ran on the road,' Aman stood up and bowed. 'Please clap for me and my alliteration,' he said.

'An ant ate Aman's hair,' Roshni said.

'As if ants eat hair,' Aman said angrily. 'The ant can eat your hair, it's much longer than mine.'

'That was just an example of an alliteration, silly boy,' Roshni grinned. 'You just need an excuse to get angry.'

Seeing that the atmosphere was getting tense, their mother said, 'Children, while I cook dinner, you all can write an essay on any topic of your choice using alliterations. The best essay will win three chocolates.'

'Why three chocolates?' Rakhee asked.

'So that whoever wins can share the prize with the others,' Mama declared. 'Sharing is caring.'

The children looked at their mother. She was an only child and often grumbled that she had wanted siblings. She constantly urged them to be grateful for each other's company.

Alliteration

is the repetition of an initial consonant sound in words that are in close proximity to each other. Sometimes these words are not consecutive. Another definition of alliteration is the occurrence of the same letter or sound at the beginning of adjacent or closely connected words. For example, Sheela wears shimmering shoes, merry men go on the merry-go-round, a worried worm sat on the window, the boy found the book boring.

Word Games

1. Write a story or a poem using alliteration.

2. Write down the names of all the objects in a room. Using an adjective for each object, describe them so that it becomes an alliteration. For example, tough table, boring bed, wonderful window, disciplined door, simple spoon, cute cup.

3. Write a story about your favourite food using alliterations.

12
Personifications are Fun

AMAN, RAKHEE AND ROSHNI sat in their mother's room playing Ludo while their Mama corrected a pile of assignments. The children loved being close to their mother, often choosing to sit in whichever room of the house she was in. Usually, from their mother's facial expression, they could guess her reaction to the assignments. Mama had a relaxed look on her face when the assignments were good and a frown when they weren't. But today Mama had just a fatigued expression on her face throughout.

An hour later, their mother stretched her neck. Then she rotated her wrists to ease the stiffness.

'Mama, how were the assignments?' Aman asked.

'Great,' she replied. 'My ninth-grade students have done a good job with personifications.'

The children exchanged puzzled looks. If the assignments were good, why hadn't she smiled? Perhaps she was just tired. She had been very busy lately.

'Personification is such a big word,' Roshni's eyes were wide. 'I'm sure it must be a complex subject.'

Mama laughed. The children watched with frowns on their faces, as though she was going to unleash a monster.

'Personification is nothing but attributing or giving a

personal nature or a human characteristic to something that is non-human,' Mama replied.

The triplets stared at each other with serious looks on their faces. They were still confused.

'My children are so puzzled,' Mama chuckled, unable to hide her amusement.

'I'll simplify it for all of you.'

'Please do, Mama,' Rakhee pleaded.

'Your explanation just went over my head,' Aman said.

'Personification means taking an object or an animal and giving it some human qualities, like emotions, thoughts and feelings,' Mama explained.

'This sounds so difficult,' Roshni said.

'I'll give you an example,' Mama elaborated. 'When someone wants to describe the wind, they can say, the wind blew over the garden rustling the leaves or it was a breezy day.'

'Yes,' Aman nodded. 'Both phrases show that the wind was blowing.'

'But when I describe it by saying, the wind whispered against my hair, I'm personifying the wind by giving it the human attribute of whispering. I can also describe it as, the wind howled through the trees, the wind swept through the garden,' Mama added.

'Hmm, interesting,' Roshni said. 'When I visited the school library yesterday, some books called out to me.'

'Perfect,' Mama said. 'You are a fast learner.'

Aman and Rakhee exchanged a look.

'I'll also give an example of personification,' Aman piped up. 'As I wrote my ten-page assignment, my hand screamed for mercy.'

'You wrote a ten-page assignment?' Roshni asked. Her eyes were as wide as saucers. Her brother hated long assignments, constantly complaining that his hand was paining and he had cramps in his fingers.

'Wow,' Mama exclaimed. 'This is super.'

Rakhee's face fell. She didn't want to be left out of this innovative game. She stared into the distance, a frown creasing her forehead. Nodding her head as though she was talking to herself, she turned to her mother.

'I'll also give it a try,' she said. 'My new shampoo made my hair dance.'

'You are always obsessed with your hair,' Aman laughed.

Rakhee was always trying new shampoos to make her hair softer. On weekends, she badgered her mom to apply warm oil on her hair and tie it in two plaits, so that it grew faster.

'Not bad,' Mama said, gathering the assignment sheets into her folder.

'The sun smiled down at us when we were doing our yoga exercises in school,' Rakhee added. Now that she had managed to give an example of personification, she had started enjoying the game.

Personification is attributing human qualities to non-human things. With personification, we emphasise a non-human's characteristics by describing it with human attributes or qualities.

BECOME A GRAMMAR GURU

'I thought the sun was scowling at us, it was so fierce. I was sweating,' Roshni grimaced. She didn't like being in the sun for too long, grumbling that it turned her skin into a tomato. She also disliked being teased about it by her siblings.

'I'll give it one more try,' Aman said. 'Rani heard the jalebi calling her name.'

Rakhee and Roshni giggled.

'Only you can understand the language of a jalebi,' Roshni said.

Aman loved all kinds of desserts, swearing that they wanted to be inside his stomach. It was a family joke that food was Aman's weakness and he could never resist a sweet dish, even if one woke him up at midnight.

Mama shook her head. 'Don't spoil the game with your arguments.'

'My window protested with a groan when I tried to open it,' Rakhee said.

'The window needs oiling,' Roshni quipped, earning a scowl from her sister.

Seeing the stern expression on their mother's face, the sisters fell silent.

'As I read a book by my favourite author, her remarkable descriptions and storytelling made the words leap off the pages, bringing the characters to life,' Roshni added. She had read her current book in three hours, completely engrossed in the story and the writing.

'Super,' Mama raised her thumb.

Walking up to the refrigerator, she took out three ice cream sticks. Handing one to each child, she said, 'A treat for all of you. You three played extremely well today.'

The triplets were surprised. Accepting the ice cream, they started eating it immediately, before their mom changed her mind.

'The ice cream begged to be eaten by us, it was calling us so loudly that we could hear it through the closed door of the refrigerator,' Roshni announced.

'Actually, even my stomach was calling the ice cream,' Aman sighed. 'I could hear it screaming for dessert for a long time.'

Mama shook her head. Aman was such a drama king and the girls were big drama queens.

Word Games and prompts

1. Personify all the objects in your school or house.
2. Tell a story about one of those objects.
3. Personify the different aspects of nature, the days of the week and the months of the year.

Writing Prompts

1. One day you wake up and find yourself in an eagle's nest. You have become small and the eagle is staring at you with hungry eyes. How did you end up in the bird's nest? Why did the eagle bring you there? Continue the story.
2. Ritika ran, chased by hundreds of rats. Some rats started flying. A few rats became larger and larger. What happens next?
3. You are travelling on a train full of animals. The animals are talking to you. You can understand them and you can also converse with them. Take the story forward.
4. The jalebi on your plate doesn't want to be eaten. The jalebi makes a deal with you. What will you do?
5. You are walking to your school, followed by a dog and a cat. Go ahead and let your imagination run wild.
6. In the library, the books are chasing you. Some books have caught hold of your arms while a few others are trying to bite you. Take yourself on a bookish adventure and complete the story.
7. The girl spoke to the tree, the tree nodded and handed her a sword. How will this story progress?
8. Personify happiness and sadness and write about your imaginary conversation with them.
9. While Ravi exercised in his garden, a bee stung him. Ravi turned into a worm. Let your imagination lead you into an adventure.

10. A crow sat on my balcony, watching me. Then the crow did something that surprised me. Allow the crow to take you on an adventure.
11. On a visit to the zoo, a tiger confides its problem to you. How will you help the tiger?
12. Write down a hundred words that come to your mind. They could be anything – a name, a place, an animal, a bird, a vegetable or a fruit. Now weave those hundred words into a story.
13. Raji is trapped inside a room with her most disliked vegetables. How will she escape?
14. Rahul wakes up in the morning and finds a snake on his bed. Take yourself on a wild adventure with the story.
15. A young vampire hates the sight of blood. The only red thing the young vampire loves is tomato sauce. Build a story around the tomato sauce-loving vampire.
16. One day Reena wakes up and realises that she can read people's minds. Can Reena have an ordinary day after this discovery?
17. While playing with your friends in the park, you see a girl sitting on a bench. Sadly, no one else can see her. Who is this girl? Why is she visible only to you?
18. Rashi finds herself in a haunted house. Why did she go there? Who does she meet?
19. On a holiday, you discover a baby dragon on the beach. The baby dragon asks you for help. What will you do?
20. Trisha finds herself teaching in the animal school. How did she end up there? What will she teach the animals?

21. The tooth fairy takes you on a magical trip to fairyland. Who are the characters you meet there? Write about your trip to fairyland.
22. One rainy night, a ghost appears in Ginny's room. Why is the ghost visiting her at night? What does the ghost want from her?
23. On a school picnic, you bump into a talking tree. What happens next?
24. I followed the ghost down the tunnel. Continue the story.
25. Carrying me in its beak, the bird soared into the sky. Where will the bird take you?
26. The day started as all Mondays do, with me chasing the school bus. What happens next?
27. The pizza on the table started talking to me. Why is food talking to you? Continue the story.
28. The bird on the tree transformed into a monkey. The monkey then climbed into my room through the window. What happens next?
29. While watching the moon from my window, I realised that I could fly. Where will you go?
30. The tree outside your house is the entrance to a magical world. Strange creatures sing and dance around it at night. Will you follow them into the tree?

Writing Space

ACKNOWLEDGEMENTS

I would never have been able to write without the support of my family. My Dad, Motilal Chhabria, forever motivating me to reach for the stars, now guiding me from the other world, unseen by human eyes. Dad taught me that impossible is a word that shouldn't figure in my life. My Mom, Sheela Chhabria, an active supporter of my writing, always encouraging me to try different genres. Thank you Mom for the encouragement. My guru, Sadguru Mata Amritanandamayi Devi, the wind beneath my wings. Lord Ganesha, for his blessings and constant inspiration.

Geeta Menon, Editor of *Children's World Magazine*, for convincing me to write the columns.

Renu Kaul Verma, for her complete belief in the stories and her excitement to publish this book. Renu, your trust and faith is so heart-warming. So is your enthusiasm. This is the fastest book deal that happened to me.

Kanagam King, for her meticulous editing.

Thank you, Kanagam, for your wonderful suggestions.

Saumya Chaudhary from Vitasta Publishing for her exceptional coordination and tireless efforts in bringing together the talents of the various people involved in the book.

Val from Aethrastic Designs for the wonderful illustrations which brought the characters alive.

Rohit, the designer for his amazing talent and creativity in designing the pages of the book. His imaginative illustrations and attention to detail have added a magical touch to every aspect of the book.

Mark Noce, author of historical novels and my critique buddy living in America, who landed on my blog one day. Ever since I have been thankful for that lucky day. Mark always gives me amazing feedback on all my manuscripts. Thank you, Mark, your insight has enhanced my book.

Author Priya Narayanan and Neetu Mishra, a teacher, for their feedback on the first few chapters.

My girl gang, Pallavi, Meera, Seema, Roopa and Anitha. You girls rock my world with your company. The sound of your laughter keeps me going.

Last but not least, you, my loving readers. Your love for my words is my oxygen. Hope you enjoy working on all the writing prompts I created.